Sim and Pim Win

By Sally Cowan

The sun was up.

Bub sat on Pim's lap.

Sim was hot!

Big Mag is not up.

Pim! I can get wet in the vat.

Sim got in the vat,
but he did not see
Kit the cat.

Kit hid in lots of logs.

As Sim got wet,

Kit ran to the vat!

Kit got up on the vat.

He jabs at Sim's legs.

Look! Pim is a jet!

Pim nips at Kit.

Kit went in the vat
and got wet!

Bub got on Sim's lap.

Kit is wet.
We win! We win!

CHECKING FOR MEANING

1. Where did Bub sit? *(Literal)*

2. Who hid in the logs? *(Literal)*

3. How was Kit feeling at the start of the story?
   How did he feel at the end? *(Inferential)*

EXTENDING VOCABULARY

vat	A *vat* is a large tub used to hold liquid. What is in the *vat* in the story? What other words could the author have used instead of *vat*?
legs	Look at the word *legs*. Which letter has been added to the base? Which word from the text can you make if you change the *e* in *legs* for an *o*?
jet	What does the author mean by *Pim is a jet!*? Do you think this is a good way to describe Pim flying?

MOVING BEYOND THE TEXT

1. How else might a bird cool off if it is hot?

2. How do you keep cool when it is hot?

3. What other animals like to hunt?

4. What was your favourite part of the story? Why?

SPEED SOUNDS

Kk	Ll	Vv	Qq	Ww

Dd	Jj	Oo	Gg	Uu

Cc	Bb	Rr	Ee	Ff	Hh	Nn

Mm	Ss	Aa	Pp	Ii	Tt

PRACTICE WORDS

lap

wet

vat

win

Kit

lots

logs

legs

lap